HUNGER FOR SALT

SAINT JULIAN PRESS

POETRY

PRAISE for ~ HUNGER FOR SALT

"The poems of Elaine Fletcher Chapman are meditations waiting for our eyes to open. A few of these poems remind me of the beautiful seashells one finds on the beach after a storm. Chapman writes from the heart reminding us to discover the strength to love. There is loss as well as celebration in *Hunger for Salt.* Here are poems Thomas Merton would tuck somewhere inside his robes. Here is the Chapman rosary for our days to come."

~ E. Ethelbert Miller
Editor, Poet Lore Magazine

"In Elaine Fletcher Chapman's *Hunger for Salt,* the hunger is palpable: for the natural world, the spiritual world, and the realm of the carnal. These powerful, well-crafted poems invite the reader into the place where these worlds meet. There is an intimacy here missing from much contemporary poetry, and intimacy is what drew me in until my hunger, like salt, dissolved."

~ Wyn Cooper

"*Hunger for Salt* is a tender evocation of the natural world. Chapman displays a poet's sensibility, a quiet attentiveness to personal wonder, intimacy and grief. The stillness of these poems exposes the refractive quality of memory and desire; it is a poignant and elegant debut."

~ J. Mae Barizo

HUNGER FOR SALT

Poems by

Elaine Fletcher Chapman

SAINT JULIAN PRESS
HOUSTON

Published by

SAINT JULIAN PRESS, INC.

2053 Cortlandt, Suite 200
Houston, Texas 77008

www.saintjulianpress.com

ISBN 13: 978-0-9986404-1-9
ISBN-10: 0-9986404-1-7
Library of Congress Control Number: 2017933844

COVER & AUTHOR'S PHOTOGRAPH
ROBERT M. CHAPMAN, II

COVER DESIGN ~ RON STARBUCK

For dear ones; Alex and Josh
And for Bob, my beloved.

CONTENTS

HUNGER FOR SALT

ONE

MORNING POEM

This morning, the air heavy with heat.
I pull back my hair and breathe.
Grasses still wet with dew.
It's good to begin the day in a field.
I say, *Are you ready?* and the dog runs
before I've even thrown the ball.
He's driven by routine. I used to say,
I've raised two children and six dogs.
This is the seventh. In a dream
several nights ago, he sweet talked me,
spoke as if I were his love. Since then,
I sweet talk him back as if he were mine.
Crazy, in the midst of loss, to be loved so.

HALF–TIME

Only daughter, my first born,
somehow I thought you were against me.
Last summer during your visit
home, you finally told me—
after disappearing for several days
with a woman you met while working
at a bar near the piers. Why was I frightened
of the distance we traded for danger?

Today, your girlfriend stood on the float
in a powder blue gown, hair sprayed,
red lipped, "Homecoming Dyke"
written on a sash across her chest.
She blew kisses. You handed out
lists of famous lesbians while standing
in a wire and paper bomb. Confusion echoed
against the crowd. The governor waved back.

BRIOCHE, LATE OCTOBER

Only days ago we sighted three bald eagles
and six blue herons in the marsh.
Sat for a time by the ocean.
It seems indulgent to want more.
I mixed the flour, eggs and warm milk.
Kneaded the dough. Let rise in the warmest room,
then braided and brushed with raw egg.
Sprinkled raw sugar. I've lost confidence.
For months, weighing each decision.
The late afternoon light lent itself
like an elixir. A promise kept.

YESTERDAY

the subject was hands,
today funerals. It's still raining
and I'm thinking about the creek:
the heron, his call
when the egret comes
too close. The tide rose because
of the storm last week and the surf high.
We're still in Ordinary Time and Basho
appeared once more. The temperature
refuses to drop.

TRAVELING THROUGH ONLEY

The landscape changes
as crops come in:
wheat, soybeans, corn.
Yesterday looking for Seaside Road,
I lost my way
because of the simple
harvesting
of grain.

FULL MOON IN DAYLIGHT

After the light brightened,
I woke desperate for a particular way:
shade among pines, creek lapping,
the shadow of an osprey,
my loved ones nearby. Time enough.
Daily embraces, kisses even. Yesterday
I read: *It is not enough to have moments of praise.*
Every gesture must become a hymn of adoration.
How does one become prayer?
I'm learning to lean in when waiting
becomes pointless. Immediate
like the row of sunflowers I pass
returning home, the merciful welcoming.

THE HOUSE IN KILL DEVIL HILLS

For Tim and Susie

On Franklin Street just off the bypass,
equal distance between sound and ocean,
sunset and sunrise, wind and wind.
Two live oaks in the back yard.
The one nearest the side door,
a sanctuary of sorts,
dark shade and deeper silence.
Two pots of pansies, random sea shells,
wind chimes and gull feathers.
Strawberries and cereal on the kitchen counter.
Fresh milk in the refrigerator.
Only room for one small bed,
a desk, a dresser, a table,
three odd chairs, and a few books.
No fear and room enough.

SEPTEMBER BEGINS

ten sun salutations

ten minutes of loving kindness

one psalm, picked randomly

this morning, one hundred and thirty one:

O, lord, my heart is not lifted up…

I have calmed and quieted my soul

one poem, not random

Whitman: *observing a spear of summer grass*

at summer's end, the marsh already turning

its autumn brown tawny

the smoke of my own breath

one hundred and eight earthly desires

the diameter of the sun

one hundred and eight times

the diameter of the earth

a few light kisses, a few embraces

a reaching around of arms

the soles of my feet

on sand, on grass, on wood

hair pinned up

arms bare,

one cup of green tea, one peach

picked randomly off the tree

older still, skin weathered

one son, one daughter

two oceans, many shores,

many river banks and creek beds

my eyes are not raised

it is not late

and time enough for my hand on your back

touching lightly the fine hair

singing of chants and hymns

one hundred messages written

on the palms of hands

AFTER JANE KENYON'S *BRIEFLY IT ENTERS, AND BRIEFLY SPEAKS*

I am the unmowed meadow,
clover and wild iris.

I am butter softening
on the pink plate.

I am the crocheted dishcloth
hanging to dry in the kitchen.

I am the lace curtain pulled to the side of the window.

When the sun rises, the small child waits until the last
moment to rise.

I am the gold poppy from California left in the pocket.

I am a crisp clean sheet.

I am the sun hiding behind thunderclouds full of lightning.

I am the heron nesting on channel marker number 35,
marsh grass on the creek bed.

I am the question behind your name.

READING LI PO BETWEEN MEALS

Write a poem
from winter's edge.

Thoughts of you unending.

A setting sun, snow covering
metaphor and excess.

No plan to go looking for such solitude.

Wake counting syllables,
wanting white hair.

LEAVING PATACARA

Somewhere outside Pittsburgh on the turnpike
near Breezewood, I left the *Therigatha,* left Patacara,
teacher of non–attachment. I bought yellow roses.

I drove to the Squirrel Hill exit and followed
Forbes to Dallas Avenue where the road divided
two cemeteries. I wanted Homewood.

I unrolled the map on which someone had drawn
a line with a pen leading to section 15–2.
It was not easy to find her

buried within circles of monuments and tombstones,
mostly granite and marble, surrounding
her with unfamiliar names. I parked the car

and walked up the slight slope to the newest marker,
where I read, Eleanor Fletcher Walters, her entire name,
unrelated and strange, written in stone.

I placed the roses to the side.
Her ashes were buried below in a black box.
I wanted to dig down, find her and then slowly

sift her ashes through my fingers
until she was scattered gently over snow,
grey against white, marking an end to our confinement.

ANTICIPATION OF BLOSSOMS

My mother knew nothing of delphinium and dahlias,
even less of lilies, those fleur–de–lis' marking north.
She resisted beauty, discouraged the ornamental.
She enjoyed a blossom only when fruit was forthcoming,
especially the pear. She surprised me by ordering daffodils,
enough for her entire front yard. Then buried each one,
the correct depth.
She told me, *I'm only interested in the anticipation of blooms.*

I didn't believe her. I thought: conversion, a door ajar,
a breeze passing through. A breeze with fragrance.
What she knew, I didn't understand.
Then her short dying, then her death,
several weeks before May, before the daffodils first blooming.

BIRTH OF A WING

Still winter and cold, off–shore wind
creating havoc, the tips of waves
scattering spray like steam from a kettle.

The gull's wing, whole and intact,
detached from its body. No blood, a clean break.
Feathers, Aegean white and undamaged.

The beach otherwise vacant. The remainder
nowhere near. Your life changed, even unrecognizable:
wind–blown, not broken. The inexplicable carnage.

RETURNING FROM THE BEACH DURING A STORM

I licked my lips and tasted salt,
blown and embedded in my skin.
I thought *not from tears this time.*

I moved the gold band
from my left to my right hand.
I wore it there for three months.

Yesterday I removed it and placed
it in my grandmother's dish on the dresser
where I noticed a few grains of sand.

REPRIEVE

Perhaps it's because today
I'm in San Francisco
and last night ate our favorite fish tacos,
Nick's way, with my son and his wife
or perhaps it's because this morning
I walked to Crissy Field and touched
the base of the Golden Gate Bridge
then came back the long way
through Fort Mason.
Perhaps it's because at the bar on Chestnut
I declined the wine labeled *Solitude*.

The light here encourages, even demands,
a different kind of reflection.
Call it refraction:

the uncomplicated grief
of my usual spring sorrow
taken over by the scent
of eucalyptus.

LIGHT FROM THE SHED

1

Sustenance arrived almost daily
in unlikely forms: books by mail,
her brother's Sunday dinners,
one shell from the South China Sea,
a stand of pines, the Atlantic Ocean,
the labyrinth at Land's End,
the Pacific Ocean,
green and brown sea glass,
a baby born the fifth day of June.

2

On Avalon Beach you can cry
and talk to yourself aloud
and everyone thinks
God has something to do with it.

3

I entered the labyrinth
and a lion entered me.

4

She has never lived where she is not known.
She walks down the street to the beach
unnoticed. The man on the porch doesn't look up.
Her face shaded by the straw hat,
a cool bottle of water in her hand.
Finally, she lives where she doesn't belong.

5

The woman was afraid
to walk into the ocean.
She thought baptism.
No one knew about the rip tide.
No one knew she entered.
She went under and stayed
until she ran out of breath.
Wet and spent, she returned
down the same road to her house
and ate cold sliced beets,
sprinkled with vinegar.
Redness stained her tongue and lips
for three sweltering days.

6

Where is goodness and grace but in the light
of a borrowed house near the shore?
The passing of light through the house
mesmerized the woman. Scared, she stared
into the dark after the light passed
before returning to its path.
She tried not to remember her other house,
the high windows, front and back, the longing
for brilliance and blindness.

NOT FAILING

Cold roasted sweet potatoes
from the Eastern Shore
on a yellow plate
beside the glass of wine.
Red pepper flakes.
Mostly, the men in my life
have failed me.
Forty years ago, in the dark,
I crouched on the stoop
of an antique shop on a busy street,
keening, not understanding
the turn my life was taking.
A stranger stopped and asked
if he could help. I answered no.
What I meant to say was yes.

LOTUS BLOSSOM

1

She was asked to live
alone by the ocean
and discover
her still point.
Only a bowl and spoon,
paper and ink.
She was asked to walk
the labyrinth, daily.
She was asked to journey
to the mountains
and follow the same path
many times. She was asked
to write the forgotten.
She was asked to sit
padmasana until she heard
the name written on her heart.

2

She wrote *alone but not lonely*.
True the moment she wrote it.
But the minute after, not true.
Again she read *lonely as an empty temple*.

Breakfast on the bench,
walking on the beach.
The other side of the bed piled with books,
magazines, yesterdays clothes.
The sound of waves breaking onshore.

UNDER THE INFLUENCE OF BASHO: MORNING PRACTICE

Moonlight on water
is a simple idea,
a system of truth.

Cooling air collects
over gravel, wet from rain.
The smell of metal.

After the predawn
rain storm, daffodils bending
away from the fence.

He closed the window
at dawn, keeping the bird's song
from disturbing her.

Clicks of a keyboard
in the next room—a quiet
clearing of the throat.

Wild pink azaleas
spot the woods where we pass by,
climbing to the summit.

TWO

HUNGER FOR SALT

This morning the air thick
with sea salt mixed with humility.
It sticks to my skin like the silence
I live with these days.
Yesterday, on my return
from the beach, a large black snake
crossed the boardwalk, traveling
from one dune to another amid
tall sea grass and oleander.
I stopped mid–step and let it pass,
surprised by absence,
alone but not lonely.

ANOTHER SPRING

Perhaps the stale grass seed
sprouted in uneven patches,
random yet patterned. The dead branches

cut in early winter, an unlit funeral pyre
on the ivy. April passes into May.
Pollen filters
a steadfast transition of early afternoon light.

How sweet familiarity is.
                                        The fallen

cherry blossoms gather a swarm of bees.
Another added year
since my mother's death.

One pink snapdragon in a small jar
on the window sill bends
toward the divine.

DEAR

Easy without you last night
and this morning through the downpour,
rain hitting the high windows hard.
I walked to the back of the house, checking
for the usual leaks and found none.
The caulking you did last weekend
saved us. The sealing of open space
between glass and rotting wood.
Not restoration but rescue.
It's what we need after all these years.
I wrote *dearest* first and then erased the word
not liking how it looked on the page.
Sorry to say, I welcomed the lack
of conversation, wondered how you felt
leaving, even for the one day.

FIRST WINTER MORNING

I woke with her words:
The memory of sun weakens in my heart.

You did not stir when I reached for you,
my hand slightly touching the blade

of your shoulder. *Darkness?*
For breakfast—tea, orange slices, day old bread.

Early rain has slowly switched to snow,
small flakes, now larger ones. Freezing

wind blows under the front door.
Why have we not kissed?

*Maybe it's a good thing I'm not
your wife.* The dried brown leaves, nearly white.

OF AUTUMN

Tonight, the veil is the thinnest.
It's easy to die, pass over
and through, talk to the dead.

I wait, offer lessons in uncertainty.
I have coals of fire in my breast.
No one answers my letters.

My day contracts as light
expands across the room.
The lace curtain lifts, settles, lifts again.

Strangers pass below. No one
dares visit. Last night's dream
contaminates my desire for rest.

PEAKS, BETWEEN RIDGES

After the aspens lost their leaves,
after the elk herd disappeared
from the field where they were grazing

several weeks, a winter storm
covered the mountain slopes with snow.
Clouds drifted below peaks, between ridges.

I watched my grown son
walk ahead up the steep incline at Snowmass
midmorning. I studied the placement

of his feet, red hair reflecting light,
the size of his hands, the bones forming his back.
I desperately wanted him to remember that his body

was lifted from my womb, evacuated
through my swollen belly. Instead, nothing.
In the distance, an occasional branch

breaking under the weight of snow.
He slowed his pace, turned and waited.
My vision blurred into the reflection of his eyes,
the unspoken clarity as crisp as the cold.

FRONTISPIECE: a Zuihitsu

If my mother were alive she would criticize my husband for
not repairing the wood around the back door and me for not
caring.

Thirty silver bells, each marking one year of marriage.

Caramelized onion soup.

Last week I wrote *footfall*. This week I read Eliot's *Footfalls echo
in the memory,/
Down the passage which we did not take / Towards the door we never
opened / Into the rose–garden.*

I reviewed a letter to the building code inspector, analyzing the
loading of spruce boards for a three–story structure in West
Ghent. It is not relevant that for fifty years a family rose
garden stood on this property. It may be relevant that over a
hundred years ago the land was most likely river–bed.

History of tea.

Crows scramble in the gutter, looking for a suitable snack.

I often think of Miriam and her field in Plymouth, before and
after the fence. Yesterday when we were talking on the phone
about meeting in Kansas City at the end of March, she saw
one coyote and a red tailed hawk.

Why did Bertrand Russell burn the letters from Vivienne
Eliot?

She is cleaning the algae from the cooler. He prepares to leave,
placing the ladder on the car.

If my mother were alive she'd keep her coat on in my house and say it was too cold to stay long.

Does one have to be on the edge of insanity? There is no easy way other than to be tormented by what is not.

The Story of My Life by Richard Jefferies.

Three reports on water intrusion and roof damage.

I sprinkled glitter in my last letter to Susan, imagining it falling on her desk or in her lap. Last night before going to bed, I found glitter on the floor in our bedroom. He seldom notices random sparkle.

In every direction, an elegy.

My search for solitude began before my conception.

Tomato and roasted red pepper soup.

The gulls moved inland.

Suppose Eliot did not destroy Emily Hale's letters?

He doesn't want to have sex at seven in the morning when he knows I am watching the clock, anxious to begin work. He says, *too mechanical.* I agree but still want to feel the weight of his body.

Early morning tea
leaves: a bird flying away
from the forest's edge.

If my mother were alive she would not like that we eat out most meals. She would still send me supermarket coupons for discounts on paper towels, toilet paper, and laundry soap. She would hate my clothes, saying *too much black. Why don't you like color?*

In August my daughter married a woman in the Shakespeare Garden in Evanston. I read Sappho: *Eros arrived from heaven wrapped in a purple mantle, / hope of love. / The love shook my heart like the wind / that falls on oaks in mountains.*

–Not wanting to leave
the house and tolerate the
sun's extreme brightness.

Now he is mounting photos for the next report. I ask, *which one?* He says *vibration in Richmond.* I watch as he runs the tip of the glue stick over the back of each print then presses it to paper. Afterward, he places the sheets aside and starts on another package of prints. I don't ask about the next ones.

Breakfast Teas: Dragonmoon, Morning Glory, Sacred Garden, Imperial Keemum.

Night sweats and broken sleep.

From where I sit, my mind lingers.
So much to learn: duende, speculation.
Bly says, *discipline and solitude.*
I say, *my hips hurt from sitting.*
A voice answers, *so take a walk.*

miasma

Roofs must withstand a much broader attack from natural forces than any other
building components. In some parts of the continental United States, roof surfaces experience annual temperature changes exceeding 200 degrees Fahrenheit and daily changes exceeding 100 degrees Fahrenheit.

Eliot writes, *I said to my soul be still, and let the dark come upon you.*
O dark dark dark.

Books stacked on the TV in our bedroom: *Soil Engineering,*
Mechanics of Materials, A Hundred White Daffodils, Heat Transfer,
Night Falls Fast.

Possibility
mingled with isolation
tenderness of sky.

Le Spectra de la rose

box of chocolates
ribbon with hearts, ripe and repeating

a moss garden

You are setting out late this morning to examine a standing
seam metal roof on a Victorian house in Franklin, ruling out
damage from the hurricane last fall.
Alone in the house for the first time in a week, I'll immediately
want to leave.

SATURDAY, WAITING

She walks into the strong wind.
The ocean, one block over.
Sand and snow sting her face.
She carries her reserves
next to her bare chest
under layers. The plaid scarf
bound tightly around her neck.
She's losing light.
Earlier, when the snow was its heaviest,
she walked from window to window.
She's weary from waiting.
Her walking, an elixir
for diminished devotion.

LEAVING THE MAINLAND

> *I know how it feels:*
> *ten thousand miles of farewell*
> *on this boat.*
>
> Li Po

Crossing the sound, belonging to no one,
watching for the north end. The ferry's wake,
its exhaust, turning the sky grey.

November.
The channel a narrow roadway for sorrow.
Bone weary from wanting. Waiting for shore.

Arriving to pine, darkened from sea spray.
Scattered broken shells. A marsh.
On the road, sand drifts.

No memory other than motion.
What is left behind is left behind.

No way to return at will.
Relief in what is known,
gathering shells, firewood before winter.

INDIAN PAINTBRUSH

Nothing in nature says no.

Charles Wright

Against the violent haze of sea–torched marsh,
scrub pine washed to its side, driven over,
months after the hurricane.
And stretches of sand misplaced in the sound.
The breach wide and wider. My half–seized,
half–singed heart gripped by what remains.
That deep red, scattered across ash,
slashing through late afternoon light.

THE NORTH END

At first I thought myself exiled. Homeless,
passing through the seasons of that first year.
I considered the weightlessness of lost belongings.
Sand and light, a way of life. Weather.
A dear friend said, *sometimes I feel connected to the earth
by a very thin thread.* I considered Blake, then Stafford.
What holds me to this place? Simple.
Basho's words: gate, interior, swept.

SEARCHING

Still trying to accept loss,
I borrow phrases from the Buddhists:
a bowl and a spoon, a single robe,
chop wood, carry water.
Name this one room studio
Holy place of contemplation.

Last week I stepped into the stone labyrinth
and immediately heard, *go home.*
For a week I asked, *Where is home?*
I open the door to hear the rain
and distant thunder. I pour
a cup of freshly brewed tea, add ice
and fresh lemon. I ask again,
Where is home?
I return to Basho,
and St. Teresa of Avila:
interior, interior.

COASTAL IMPORTS

After two years, I still return
to my old neighborhood
for car repairs: Coastal Imports.
I'm the one who moved closer
to the coast where wind grabs
my storm door and slams
it against the outside wall, repeatedly,
if I'm not careful. The salt air
corrodes the undercarriage
and rusts the frame.

The motor mounts broken
and the oxygen sensor burned out.
I can't remember who I was
before I left the marriage.

THREE

FALL MORNING

I begin my day in light
with sweetness from the summer peach
sliced into the blue speckled bowl
covered white with milk.

Lament, no longer necessary,
having grieved for all I know and don't know.
That particular prayer for the dead unsaid
for months, even in deep sleep.

In a minute the rose wood incense will burn down,
ashes left in a line. Later
I will leave the house, return past dark
to discover an entire river running through this room.

THIRD SUNDAY IN JULY

Yesterday I allowed
you to wash
each foot in turn
with the mildest of soaps.
After you left, I placed
the lapis stone
shaped like a heart
on the prayer, to hold it down.
Thank you for bringing
me to this place
of surrender, hopefulness.
Today, our Sabbath
separation.
You in the pulpit,
me at my desk,
doing work
we are called to do.

WORK

I'm afraid to say we work in unison.
Once before that notion betrayed me.
Once I found comfort in double solitude.
I won't allow myself that sanctuary, that vision.
No. For us it is the mystical third, not the double.

LATE MARCH CROSSING THE BAY

What I noticed on the trip over:
the green heron, a pelican, sea gulls,
waves before the second tunnel,

roadside daffodils, chilly air.
We sat at your kitchen table for lunch.
We lay down in your bed. I fell

asleep in your arms. When we woke,
I could not move. At dinner you cried,

remembering the sound of your daughter
coming through the front door of your old house.
Sitting by the window, we lost dusk.

On my return I noticed: the nearly full moon
and clear sky, stars, a lone farmhouse
with a light in each window,

 water moving below the bridge.

END OF SUMMER

Near Bloxum we turned right on Masons Road.
Not as far as the railroad tracks.
We found a vineyard carved from a cornfield.
You liked Red Kiss and I chose Chardonnay.
We sat at a table outside where trellises
covered with flowering vines surrounded us
and three dogs slept under our feet.
We were already intoxicated by the sight
of one another, as if we suddenly surfaced
from the bottom of the sea, gasped for air
and realized we survived being held under
against our will. What could we do but reach
for each other, notice how we were changed:
your eyes greener, my hair longer.

SOLITUDE

How fitting, on the eve of my marriage, a full moon.
I'm sitting at my desk in the new study.
My library lined on shelves behind me. The books
that have seen me through, the ones packed
and unpacked, my companions, my comfort:
Kenyon, Rilke, Wright, Williams, Dickinson,
and especially Woolf. Virginia, her insistence,
her turmoil, her clarity. The Angel in the House
reminding me of my place at the table.
Until now, I never knew what it meant: *The Beloved*.
There is little point thinking about time wasted.

STEADY RAIN

His body was found after five days,
decayed at the table he used for a desk.
Bent over that same table we bought
when I was nineteen. Still unfinished.
I received the call. I said, *break in the back door.*
In turn, I called our children.
The cops and old neighbors waited in the front yard.
A two hour drive.
I entered his study after six years.
Miasma of misery. Mercy.
He never asked for forgiveness, his many transgressions.

ANOTHER ATTEMPT AT SILENCE

I'm deep in silence. This time
not invisible where the body
doesn't count. No, I'm counting
on hips, heart, feet, memory.
In this silence I exist. Strong
winded force borne from the
coolness of fall. Burning off,
bearing down silence.
Borne from experience,
bothered by little.
Not a holding back silence.
Not holding in either.
A listening silence: Dishes
being washed, bird song,
bricks being laid in the church
yard next door.
Traffic on Market Street.
A choice. Not containment.
Not contamination.
Lips not moving. Stillness.
My breath beside, not inside.
An iridescent silence. Not silent.
Unbound, ash blond strands
covering my eyes. I can see
clearly type of silence. Divisible
by the number of days left in summer.
The water temperature warmer
than air type of silence.
Not exhaustion. Not embellishing.
Not the first time nor the last.

BEYOND

(Bennington, VT)

This morning, Prometheus
and *all suffering is holy.*
My bare feet on the cold floor.
Waking before first light.
Temperatures rising today to balmy.
The odor from the burst pipes
earlier in the week, dissipated.
Now the singular fragrance of orange peel.

PILGRIMAGE

Today the sky is mostly grey,
some stratified blue just above
the tree line. A single robin
sounds his morning call.
Is perpetual wandering necessary?
First, the neighbor's pond,
then our un–weeded flower bed,
next the long lawn, not quite a field.
I read *rule of thirds, turning away*
from things as they are.
The unmade bed. Dirty laundry piled
in a basket by the closet. Bills unpaid.
Suitcase still packed from last night's commute.
No groceries other than bread.
A season of surprise, a Thursday
and I'm home. Church bells across
the street ring the noon hour.
That white steeple, that spire.

COMMUTE

A heavy frost this morning and the full moon still up.
I stayed inside, looking from kitchen window to yard.
My kitchen window. *My* kitchen table. *My* teacup in hand.
Yesterday I worked all day knowing I was almost done.
Gone for several days and nights. Then the drive
in the dark over and under the bay. Back across.
It should be routine by now, this coming and going.
For now I want to sleep at night in *my* bed, with *my* husband,
with *our* dog. I want my husband's sleeping breath to wake me.
I want him to roll over, let his hand find my back.
When I wake in the middle of the night, I want to know where
I am.

REVELATIONS

Each week, as I return, the sun is lower.
Last night I noticed a thin fog over the fields
then the blue moon.
So much changes in one night.

In a dream my dead father called on the phone.
The next day his wife discovered my missing typewriter
buried in the back of his closet.
Did he steal it from my house
when he attempted to retrieve
my mother's belongings after her death?
He secretly replaced the items,
my brother told me later.
I never imagined the typewriter stolen.
It had simply disappeared.

May I live a life of ease.
Regardless of that layer of fog, the blue moon,
Loving–kindness meditation,
I've given it my best
and I'm not at ease.

SABBATH #55

My husband takes his breakfast plate
and places it in the sink. Clears the table.
Closes the dining room blinds, empties trash
from each room every Saturday into a large plastic bag,
carries the old bulletins collected on the dining table
to his study upstairs, matches his unmated socks,
sleeps with covers tucked under his chin.
Combs his hair with a blue plastic comb he keeps
on the bathroom counter beside his razor.
We are newly married. Almost one year.
Only this morning I referred to our house as *home*.
Before sleep, he often fingers my hair.

FOUR

SATURDAY MORNING IN APRIL

I'm lucky. I have morning light
and rose incense from the monastery
above Woodstock. It's spring and I'm home.
The last two nights I've slept in my own bed
with my husband, touching him to locate myself:
a forearm, his hand, a thigh. Leg against leg.

Forget the long passage. Forget the deaths, the dying.
Forget nights away. Forget missing the roses
first blooming, the iris, creek smells.

I've climbed the stairs.
Looked out over the marsh.
Taken to heart loss, love.
I'm waiting for the chariot to cross the sky,
the ferry to arrive from Tangier. Too many
launches have been missed.

STILL MOURNING

Love the white with red
centers, deep in peony
season, tears held back

JULY, LAST OF THE MONTH

Last nights rain left mist
in the trees this morning
as I drove the country road
where a farmer was already
on his tractor pulling
a trailer with rusted blades behind.
My arms still sore
from lifting my own weight.

THREE MINUTES BEFORE LEAVING

Linen ironed, pineapple cut and placed
in the plastic container. And emerald earrings
bought long ago. It's Tuesday.
It doesn't matter if I'm ready.
I must go, cross the bridge, work.
This morning at six, the mirror fell
off the dresser and didn't break.
We want what we want.
The necessary practice of parting.
Cold tea. One tongued kiss.

THURSDAY, MORNING

Last week at Assateague we saw a gull
with a fish in his claws flying to shore
along with four brown pelicans, circling.
Last night after dinner you drew me close.
Earlier we closed the windows to the heat.
Today I tried three times to pray.
Where is the sacred text I'm tied to?
We walked, moving our arms and legs in unison.
Our pilgrimage to the ocean. Holy salt.

SELF PORTRAIT AFTER BREAKFAST

Fresh eggs and bacon, peach preserves
from a recent stay at Holy Cross Monastery

and toast with butter. Asked
to sit quietly until served. Shades shut

against summer heat. Green tea.
Gentle gestures: cloth napkins, the Haviland china.

One has to do without, perhaps even suffer
an extended time to imagine simple kindness.

And the task of receiving a mystery
requires diligence, a nascent faith.

Disciple of hospitality. Reverence.
And she said: *Behold. The winter has passed.*

AS IF

Marsh stench.
Sea grass, mud, uprooted tree stumps.
Thousands of waterfowl.
Crabs, clams, oyster beds.
Wetlands. Following the road
around Wallops, the straightaway
to Chincoteague. We take
little other than towels and water,
pleased like we escaped, without notice.
Like it's a secret we're leaving the mainland.
Like Li Po, like Basho. The very act a prayer.
Like we're racing to save our lives.
Like we can't breathe until we arrive.
Begging for respite, restoration.
Like our souls won't survive,
Like our skin might peel off.
Windows open to the wind.
Already sea salt gathers on our upper lips,
in our hair. I tie mine back with a cotton scarf
to keep loose strands from further whipping my face.
Simple flagellations. Our reward for sacrifice.
Sanctified. Like Saint Francis we left at the front door.
Like Saint Teresa, like Rumi's Birdsongs.
Like blood.

AFTER THE HURRICANE, LATE FALL

With the storm came resignation.
Last week *refuge* written in the text
twice. I don't come to stillness easily.
Wind driven rain, now cold,
precursor to winter, weeks away.
On the Eastern Shore,
high water. The full moon
making matters worse. Finally,
Lectio, Meditatio, Oratio, Contemplatio.
No crossing over the bay,
no sounds other than wind,
no voices other than the Divine.

Only recovery, removing debris
from tide stained shores.

BEFORE THE LENTEN SERVICE AT NOON

And this morning the word *Selah*.
Hebrew for liturgical direction,
to pause, rest. An interlude. Appears
three times in Psalm Thirty–two,
the one I'm to read today.
Blessed is he whose transgression is forgiven.

A month before he died,
my father said he was sorry.
It was the ninth of June, a Saturday
as I was leaving his house, he said it:
"I didn't mean to hurt you."
Called me by my family name.   *Selah*

Our last conversation, our first in years.
I said, "It's okay, Dad. I know."   *Selah*

For once, he meant what he said.
The cure, instantaneous.
Conversion. Love at the bottom of the river,
on the other side.

This morning we woke early.
Frost overnight made the ground hard.
Seven months since my father's death.
And shout for joy, all ye that are upright in heart.
Forgiven. Forgiven. And forgiven.

Selah

TOWARD CONTENTMENT

Today spring birds return
or is it that windows are open
and I can finally hear their songs.
It's where I begin, pick up the thread
left days ago, years ago.
I realize my *divine discontent*
never disappeared. I'm unchanged.
We repeat aloud, *small corrective actions*.
Yesterday the moon, closest to earth
and this morning, a dolphin
in the creek, feeding. I'm always hungry
for one thing or another: bird song, time,
my husband's voice, words on the page
in the right order. Reconciliation.
Not with others but with myself.
A settling with dissatisfaction.
A bald eagle sighted last week
on a bleached branch should be enough.

HE MARKED MY BODY

When the honey
in his mouth

entered mine,
I fell

backwards
and he caught me,

honey
dripping

down
my neck,

and he kissed me
clean.

UPON MY RETURN: A COMMONPLACE BOOK

FEBRUARY 4

Merton waits in his small cabin
for the revelation of Christ,
the mystery of iniquity as the deep
bell rings sending that holy sound
through the little cedars. I'm in
an open field waiting, watching,
listening to the geese cross
the open sky in an arrow.
Still steeped in cold–damp,
the creek thaws each day
then freezes again at night.
I'm waiting, not for Christ, nor Buddha.
I'm waiting to hear a strong voice
with clear directions: Do this,
now do that. Like God gave Moses.
I will follow the advice. I promise.
I'm wondering if at this juncture
did I not miss the instructions or understand
the translation? The grackles arrive
by the thousands. Townspeople stop putting
out birdfeed because they eat everything in sight
and then fly on. Yesterday the birds turned
the cloudy sky black at noonday when
the bells across the street marked the hour.

FEBRUARY 8

It's good to travel away from farmland into the city
for a fancy lunch in a fine dining room:
Grilled tenderloin, roasted asparagus, champagne.
We remember something about ourselves
before we moved to the country. We walked
the long walk to the capital where today they voted
to change the laws concerning *unnatural acts*.
We heard the legislator say adults have rights
in the privacy of their bedrooms. *Unnatural acts*
left undefined. It seemed everyone agreed.
My husband gave the opening prayer.
I didn't say, *Hey, what about separation of church and state?*
No, I sat in the designated seat and everyone in the chamber
knew I was the wife of the preacher. A smile on my face,
a lacy scarf, soft blouse and sweater, proper shoes.

MARCH 27

Last week two bald eagles
perched in a field as I passed.
Upon my return they were gone.
As if I imagined them sitting there
on frozen ground. Just after seeing
the tundra swans swimming at Assateague
and the day before, white snow geese.
Driving the same farm roads,
moving in light, then shade.
Yesterday high winds kept
mail from being delivered.
The fields still frozen, making the turning
of soil difficult. We want to go home.
But where? Ice still lines the creek.
The marsh, still brown. I'm mostly silent.
Waiting for the sun to warm us.

MARCH 31

Small scraps of paper with names and numbers,
photos from the wedding in San Francisco.
Bookmarks sent from Argentina in an envelope
from the Hotel Danieli on Riva Degli
Schiavoni, Venice. Not just memories,
but what holds a life. Worn notebooks.
Notes about 20 miles of ribbons in Grace Cathedral.
Prayers, hopes and wishes written on the red ones.
Conjure and truth and E.D.'s *life is a spell So*
exquisite, every–thing conspires to break it.
The second half of Lent and this morning Merton's
The return is not going back. Beginning soothes us.
Notes written on old postcards from Sacramento
and The Fermilab in Batavia, Illinois.
The consequences immense.
That broken collarbone. *Shunyata*
and eighty–four thousand open doors.
One organic orange, cut in four sections.
Golden raisins. High winds from the Northeast.

MARCH 29

I'm reminded that on this date
Virginia Woolf put on her coat,
walked to the river and placed pebbles
in her pockets before she waded in.
I'm surrounded by water.
A sad day, losing her like that.
She wrote, *without money freedom is impossible.*
Recently I discovered my own windfall.
Enough to begin without obligations.
Not inheritance, not legacy.
Not a buy in, not a pay off.
But a message sent directly from the other side.
I'm to write *the accumulation of the unrecorded life.*
I am that august woman, having waited
impatiently for this unexpected season.

APRIL 2

Merton gave little inspiration this morning.
I turned to Bly and then Wright.
Those sunflowers bending toward mercy.
Those blessings and bodies into blossom.
Another funeral today. A suicide. And yesterday
a man I did not know sitting across from me
at the funeral luncheon who at the mention
of my father's name, being caught off guard,
cried. Perhaps he was already overcome
with sadness. But my father's name brought the tears.
How the man had been saved. How my father always listened.
How he always fought for the underdog.
I heard myself speaking plainly of his meager beginnings.
Supporting himself by playing saxophone in dance bands.
The dark blue velvet lining the case. The reed damp with spit.

APRIL 7

Exhaustion and a pulled thigh muscle
has me consulting Burton's
The Anatomy of Melancholy,
looking for a cure.
He's been helpful before
with the Miseries of Scholars.
Not that I'm a scholar.
But the advice is solid.
Has she broken open street–doors?
Has she torn any clothes?
I can't say I've done either. But I have repeated
fuck and damn it to hell.
My mother used to say damn it to hell
and we knew she was really mad.
No pastoral scene today. Just heavy rain,
a muddy field.

MAY 1

After the last few days of steady downpour,
the wheat has grown so I can no longer see
around the curve. It is the spring crop here
on the Shore. Recently a young woman told
me the memory of a combine moving across
the field helps her sleep. I'm moving from
this place in a month. I will miss the rotation
of crops: wheat to soybeans to corn and back
again. I will miss the church bell across the side
street sounding noon and six. I'm taking all
things in as if it were a last breath, a dream
I must remember, like the combine
crossing the field, like green wheat.

WHAT THE WATERMEN CALL THIS PLACE: THE WEST SIDE

Three snapping turtles laid eggs
in the backyard the week we moved
into the new parsonage.
Foliage keeps the reservoir distant.
Only if we stand can we see water.
No salt and no tide.
A light rain and gray sky.
An owl lives close by in the elm.
We live on the West side now.
Me like a bird wanting an aerial view.
The mouth of the York River,
a twenty minute drive down a dismal highway
with junk yards and scrap metal repositories
on either side. I will never give up
longing for both oceans.

ABOUT THE AUTHOR

Elaine Fletcher Chapman (formerly Elaine Walters McFerron) lives on the West side of the Chesapeake Bay. She holds an MFA from The Bennington Writing Seminars, Bennington College where she has worked on the staff since 1999. She founded The Writer's Studio where she teaches poetry and nonfiction, provides editing services and organizes poetry readings and writing retreats. Her poems have been published in *The Tishman Review*, *The EcoTheo Review*, *The Cortland Review*, *Connotation*, *The Sun*, *Calyx*, *Poet Lore*, *5AM*, *Salamander*, and others. She was guest blogger on The Best American Poetry Blog. Green River Press published her letterpress chapbook, *Double Solitude*. She writes nonfiction as well as poetry.

For further inquiry: www.elainefletcherchapman.com

NOTES

Leaving Patacara is in memory of my mother, Eleanor Rue Fletcher Walters (1923-1994). Patacara (6th c. BC) was one of the most powerful personalities in the early Buddhist community. She lost her husband and her children and then lost her mind, which led her to Buddhism. The *Theragatha* translated as Verses of the Elder Nuns is an early sacred Buddhist text of short poems that were recited in India around 600 B.C.

In **Reading Li Po Between Meals** the line *Thoughts of you unending* is taken from the poem *Thoughts of You Unending.* The line *No plan to go looking for such solitude* is quoted from the poem *In the Stone Gate Mountains, Gone Looking For Yuan Tan-Ch'Iu.* Both poems can be found in *The Selected Poems of Li Po* translated by David Hinton and published by New Directions in 1996.

The line in **Another Spring,** *How sweet Familiarity is,* a quote from Charles Wright's poem, *Looking Around II* in his book *A Short History of the Shadow* published by Farrar, Straus, Giroux in 2002.

There are many references and quotes by Thomas Merton. During the time of composition, *A Year with Thomas Merton: Daily Meditations from His Journals* written by Thomas Merton, selected and edited by Jonathan Montaldo published by Harper Collins in 2004 were read and used extensively as daily devotional and poems were written in the tradition of midrash.

Poems influenced directly: **Beyond; Morning, Influenced By Full Moon; Pilgrimage; Summer Heat; After The Hurricane, Late Fall; Upon My Return, February 4; Upon My Return, February 6, Upon My Return, March 31.**

Of Autumn pays homage to John Keats. Keats died at the age of 25 from tuberculosis in Rome on February 23, 1821. He wrote his last letter on November 30, 1820. In a letter to Charles Brown dated November 1, 1982 from Naples, Keats wrote: *Oh, Brown I have coals of fire in my heart.* All Saints Day or All Hallows is celebrated between October 31 and November 1. It is believed that the bond between the living and the dead is closest that day.

In **First Winter Morning** the lines *The memory of sun weakens in my heart, Darkness?*, and *Maybe it's a good thing I am not your wife* is taken from *Twenty Poems* by Anna Andreevna Akhmatova translated from Russian by Jane Kenyon with Vera Sandomirsky. Dunham co-published by Nineties Press & Ally Press in 1985. Robert Bly encouraged Jane Kenyon to pursue translation.

Frontispiece: a Zuihitsu employs the Japanese literature genre. A Zuihitsu consists of loosely connected personal essays and fragmented ideas that typically respond to the writer's surroundings. They generally focus on personal writing and contemplation. Dedicated to Donald John McFerron, PE (1947-2011).

In **Before The Lenten Service At Noon** the lines, *Blessed is he whose transgression is forgiven, You are a hiding place for me, And shout for joy, all ye that upright in heart* and *Selah* are quotes from Psalm Thirty–Two.

In **Self Portrait After Breakfast** the line *Behold. The winter is over* is taken from the biblical text of the Song of Solomon, Chapter two, Verse eleven.

And with deep gratitude to Liam Rector, Jason Shinder, Lucie Brock-Broido, Alice Mattison, Ed Ochester, Lynne Sharon Schwartz, Miriam O'Neil, Catherine Parnell, JoeAnn Hart, Julie Walls, Wyn Cooper, Janet Sylvester, and Scott Cairns. And to the Bennington Writing Seminars community for sustenance and safe haven for a number of years. To Jackson Wilder McFerron, Emma Fletcher McFerron, and Caroline Gailey McFerron who fill my life with joy and inspiration. And finally, to Tammy Estep for Divine Intervention, a lesson in surrender resulting in an unexpected gift of contemplative time.

ACKNOWLEDGMENTS

The author wishes to thank the editors of the journals in which theses poems appeared. A number of the poems were published under the name Elaine Walters McFerron.

The Tishman Review: "Sabbath #55"

The EcoTheo Review: Faith & Ecology in Conversation: "Yesterday"

Cortland Review: "Brioche, Late October;" "Morning Poem"

Calyx, A Journal of Art and Literature by Women: "Half–Time"

5AM: "Reading Li Po Between Meals;" "Anticipation of Blossoms;" "Returning from the Beach During a Storm;" "The House in Kill Devil Hills"

Salamander: "Leaving Patacara"

Connotation Press: "Birth of a Wing"

Poet Lore: " Traveling through Onley"

SPACES Lit Magazine (Online): "As If;" "Morning, Influenced by Full Moon;" "Before the Lenten Services at Noon;" "Pilgrimage;" "After the Hurricane, Late Fall"

CPSIA information can be obtained
at www.ICGtesting.com
Printed in the USA
BVOW09s0943130517

484010BV00001B/67/P